# GET OUT OF YOUR WAY

## Success is right behind you.

**W9-DJL-796**

Marilyn and Larry Singer
*Contributing Editor*
Harrison Singer

**Outskirts Press, Inc.**
**Denver, Colorado**

*Dedicated to our parents, Clifford and Dorothy Porter and Israel and Fay Singer, who have been the supreme influences in our lives; to our children, Marcy, Jodi and Harrison, who are constant reminders of how good life is; and to our friends who are there for us no matter what. We thank you.*

---

*For more information on the Get Out of Your Way seminar series contact On Your Way training at 716-570-8926 or go to Getoutofyourwaynow.com and click Contact Us.*

# Foreword

We originally began this book wanting to share thoughts with our children, family and friends, many of whom have helped and guided us through most of our lives. Many of the thoughts are not original and have been gathering in our heads for years as a result of attending seminars and trainings, studying the writing of some of the most influential motivators of our time, teaching thousands of individuals how to attain financial and time freedom and teaching hundreds of students at State University of New York at Buffalo, preparing them for what lies ahead. Original material we have created was, we are sure, influenced enormously by others.

Where we have been able to identify the originator of concepts or thoughts that we offer herein, we have given them credit. Many others' thoughts have sprung from sources our feeble mental equipment simply can't recall: yet the words have inspired and motivated us and we could not exclude them. Therefore, you will see "unknown" as the source, rather than our taking credit. For those whose teachings have made such an impact on us that we think their thoughts are our own, we apologize for not giving due credit and thank you for your profound impact on our lives. If any of our readers know whose words are uncredited, we would greatly appreciate enlightenment.

Get Out of Your Way is not intended to be a scientific work; it is simply a layman's interpretation of decades worth of listening, learning, studying and self-evaluation. We are grateful for the wisdom of the many incredible individuals who have helped us, challenged us, coached us, sometimes dragged us and virtually pushed us to do what they knew we could do.

We needed that!

# Contents

*Long-winded writers I abhor*

*And glib, prolific chatters;*

*Give me the ones who tear and gnaw*

*Their hair and pens to tatters:*

*Who find their writing such a chore*

*They only write what matters.*

*–GROOKS*

# Introduction

## You Are In Your Way

Many of us have read books, listened to tapes, attended seminars and watched TV shows in an effort to improve ourselves, become corporate leaders, move forward within our lives, and attain the dreams we think are unattainable. Marilyn and I are two such people who have experienced all of these opportunities to advance in our personal and professional lives. We have also taught how to find, grasp and implement these opportunities for more than 20 years. We understand these opportunities have value only if they are implemented within our lives.

Marilyn and I have studied this for years and have identified the one common thread that is present in all our successes and all our failures: us. We are always there. And, yes, **we are in the way** of our own success, happiness, and eventual advancement.

And now, the time has come for you to get out of your own way!

Get Out of Your Way is intended for all of you who have stopped short of achieving your goals, your dreams, for those of you who are dissatisfied or frustrated by your current position in life. Read this book. Keep this book. And then read it again. Pay it forward by recommending this book to others who you think would benefit from it. You and they will learn how to:

- Get out of the way of your success;
- Follow the path to your dreams;
- Turn fears into excitement;
- Become the person you've always wanted to be;
- Change your attitude from a wannabe to "I am."

We are offering you five easy steps to success:

Step 1: Get Out of Your Way
Step 2: Find Your Way
Step 3: Be On Your Way
Step 4: Sidestep Obstacles in Your Way
Step 5: Stay Out of Your Way

This book is a unified collaboration of our combined experiences and perspectives.

This book is for those of you who haven't accomplished what you want and feel someone or something is always getting in your way. It is also for those who have reached heights beyond their dreams and who, as most of us do, **want still more**. Take our word for it - there is nothing wrong with that. We've been poor, and we've had money; and having money is definitely more fun. We've each been lonely, and we've each enjoyed loving relationships; and having and giving love in your life is infinitely joyful. We've had illness as well as great health; once again, health wins. And science has proven that your mental attitude will affect your physical health. We choose health.

If we have your attention, keep reading. If not, you can, as a famous motivator once said, *"Keep on doing what you're doing, and you'll continue to get what you've got."* In order to change your *results*, you must first change your actions. In order to change your *actions*, you must change how you *think*. This book addresses that mindset and how it affects your eventual results.

Thanks for reading on; or better yet, thank yourself.

Marilyn and I have spent over 70 collective years in the advertising business and many more years guiding people in finding businesses that allow them to experience their dreams. One day, as we were reflecting on the joy in our life, it hit us that we were living what we had learned and taught from our own experiences. We realized that we're direct, vivid examples of the teachings we've studied and subsequently, taught others. However, we do remember, during this continual process, getting bogged down in theory or with words that would send us scrambling for our dictionaries. We have always felt that there must be a better way; thus, the development of this "Get Out of Your Way" self-help book.

Our actual experiences as trainers, mentors, advertising professionals, college professors, husband/

wife, father/mother, son/daughter, brother/sister, and friend, all led to the conclusion that achieving your goals boils down to five simple words: "Get Out of Your Way" or GOOYW for short. We think this is a rather amusing acronym, because when you are in your way, life gets gooey, sticky, frustrating, clouded, complicated, and the list goes on.

### LARRY SHARES:

*My first experience on how to get out of your own way was when I was 14 years old. My dad came home and told us his company had just lost their biggest account. He then said, "Let's go, we're going out." My dad took my mom, little brother, and me to an auto dealership and bought three brand new Buicks: a blue one for his father, a green one for his brother (who were both in business with him) and a gray one for us. I remember saying, "Dad you just lost your biggest account. Why are we doing this?" And he said, "Things will get better." It took me a long time before I understood what he already knew. He knew that if he dwelt on the loss of this account, it wouldn't be productive: in fact, it would drain his energy. My dad knew it would be easy for him to get in the way of his moving forward; if he allowed himself to become depressed and disappointed. Instead, my dad chose to focus on a better future for him and his family, and the eventual outcome was exactly that! Every time we got into our new Buick my dad would smile. It was a symbol of what he could do and a reminder to him to keep doing the best he was able to do every day.*

*I'll never forget that day; however, I didn't realize the huge impact it made on my life until many, many years later. I learned you can't let the set-backs slow you down.*

So, dear readers, we hope you enjoy this book, and we hope we can help you move forward into the life you want and deserve.

*Marilyn and Larry Singer*

Step 1:
# Get Out of Your Way

## A. The Common Denominator

What is the common denominator to all your failures, successes, hesitations, procrastinations, and lost opportunities?

Think about this as you go through your day. When things don't go exactly as you planned or would like; when things go wrong; when life moves more slowly than expected…what is the **constant**? Do you blame it on not having the time or the money, or that your family stopped you? Perhaps it's too cold or too hot? Perhaps the reason things are going badly is because you're overweight? Underweight? Perhaps you're having a bad hair day? Write down, right now, the excuses you create for yourself.

_____

_____

_____

_____

Think about all those opportunities that came along that you chose not to pursue. Perhaps, you asked your friends and family, who were in the same poor personal or financial shape as you, their opinion. Maybe they told you, *"That will never work,"* *"Don't fall for that,"* *"You're going to be rich?"* or *"You're just fine without that."*

The constant in all your life decisions - good and bad - is that **YOU are always there**. Events in your life are so diverse that it would be impossible to find another constant.

As hard as it may seem, though many people complain about their various circumstances, most people are comfortable with where they are, because it's *familiar* to them. This, in turn, means they're comfortable where *you* are because you pose no threat of doing "better" than they. Think about it: if you go higher up the ladder, their status quo looks lower on that same ladder. Trying something new and breaking out of your comfort zone is a threat to most people. Most friends and family won't encourage you to try anything new, and you'll wind up staying exactly where you are: complacent, unhappy, dissatisfied or *un*satisfied and wishing you could move forward with your life.

Woody Allen once said, *"90% of life is just showing up."* Take a moment and think about that. Could a reasonable first step for you be simply showing up?

Do you know that 96% of the wealth in this country is in the hands of 2% of the population? And, consider this: if all the money in our country was distributed equally, like in a Monopoly game, in 3-5 years, the money would be right back in the 2%'s hands. So what does this have to do with anything? What this means is that even if you suddenly found yourself wealthy, skinny, in a higher paying job, holding an influential public office, being a rock star, or any other wild dream, the chances of your maintaining that status would be very low. Why? Because you haven't changed your mindset. When the going gets tough, we tend to scurry back to our comfort zone because we don't give ourselves a chance to experience things that are new and "scary."

If we are overweight, we may not know what being skinny feels like. If we are a smoker, we probably don't remember what being a non-smoker felt like. We avoid the unknown and revert to that with which we are familiar.

In most cases, you're afraid of trying new things; and, therefore, you will slip right back into your comfort zone. You see, learning how to have and hold onto wealth and happiness is both a mindset and a skill set.

Logic tells us that if you're always there when things go wrong or right, then you're the one who must take the credit or the blame. Change the word blame to responsibility. It's a little easier to swallow if you rename it, isn't it? The point is you must hold yourself accountable if you want to affect change.

**You** are the common denominator when you don't achieve what you want to achieve. Therefore, I am telling you, **right now: Get Out of Your Way.** You heard me right. Get out of the way of your own success. You're probably saying to yourself, *"Fine, sounds great. But how do I do that?"*

## B. Resisting the Programming

We have paradigms, habits, comfort zones, into which we retreat, even when we're given opportunities to improve ourselves. This results in keeping us exactly where we are, even though we believe we want to improve our situation. We consistently get in our own way.

We have grown up with routines and rules that we've embraced (or resisted) from parents, teachers, friends and the media. It's okay to do this, not okay to do that. I'm not saying that everything we've been taught is wrong; however, we rarely focus on and re-evaluate the rules by which we conduct our lives.

We are on "autopilot" – pre-programmed; yet, the world around us is changing and will continue to change. When we say resist programming, we are not suggesting you reject everything. Resist means to take a closer look before you make the same decisions you have always made. Resist rejecting opportunities because they look different from those with which you are accustomed.

Unlock your mind and really examine your

possibilities. Will this mean that you may have to act differently than you have in the past? Yes. Is that a good thing? Well, of course it is.

A friend called me one day and told me about an opportunity in network marketing. I immediately said, *"Is that pyramid stuff?"* He responded, *"Yes,"* and I said, *"No way."* You see, my thinking for years had been that this type of business was illegal, and no one except the people who started it made money. I think I may have gotten that idea YEARS ago, from Glen Turner and his "Dare to Be Great" business: that was my thinking, my perception, and I was not about to change it. Fortunately for me, my friend was persistent and insisted that I at least try to get off my position and try something different. He reminded me that unless I had the experience how would I know? I was getting in my own way of looking at an opportunity for no concrete reason except that it was what had been programmed into me; and I was resisting changing my thoughts.

Reluctantly, I decided to seek out additional information, this time with an open mind so I could absorb the information I was receiving. Sometimes we ask questions yet never hear the answers because we've already made up our minds. We ask questions to pacify someone else or appear polite, but we're not listening or interested in the answer.

Well, this time I decided to do something I usually

don't do, which was to really listen. And when I did, I changed my thoughts - resulting in my actions changing; which, resulted in my income changing. That was a very good thing, as Martha Stewart says.

## C. Adjust Your Attitude

Now, are you ready to re-adjust your attitude? I hope so, because that's what you need to do in order to Get Out of Your Way. When you look at the word attitude, many people associate a negative connotation to it, like "He has an attitude." However, I want you to associate attitude positively, by putting on your positive glasses whenever you see the word attitude. For example, Marilyn's father, who was a decorated bomber pilot in WWII, always lived by the following:

### *"Attitude determines altitude."*

What is your attitude toward yourself? Before you read any further, take a minute to write down what you think of yourself. And don't forget to be brutally honest. Do you think you're smart, dumb, funny, aggressive, angry, distrustful? There is no wrong answer.

_____

_____

_____

What did you write? Is it *"I'm not good enough,"* *"I'm too good for them,"* *"People are always picking on me,"* or, *"If only I had the money, then I could do that."* Maybe you wrote, *"I'm good enough."* Why would you settle for 'good enough?' We believe 'good enough' is **not** good enough: you deserve to allow yourself to excel...to "be all that you can be" as the Army recruiters suggest.

Where do you think these opinions of yourself are created? Well, they come from you. No, really, they don't come from anyone else but you. Eleanor Roosevelt once said, *"No one can make you feel inferior without your permission."* Think about that: it's so true. Why do you criticize yourself for what you've done? Your biggest champion and supporter should be YOU. If you don't believe in yourself and support yourself, who will? What is past is past. What you've done, how you've felt, what you've believed, is all past. The future is now. All you really have is right now. Spending valuable time and energy fretting about the past is a waste of time, and speculation about future obstacles can be a self-fulfilling prophecy. Make NOW the best it can be; make NOW your priority. What you think and do **now** determines your future.

So, remember, what is the common denominator to all your failures, successes, hesitations, procrastinations, and all your lost opportunities? **You.**

In order to move forward, you must first recognize the status quo: you must acknowledge that you've been in your way. Don't *blame* yourself or other people. Just accept responsibility. Don't *blame* your circumstances. After all, you're the one who chose to believe what other people think about you; and you're the one who chose to be complacent in your circumstances.

Robert Allen once said, *"You wouldn't worry about what others think of you if you knew how little they think of you."* I love that. We are all self-centered, so we think that people spend so much time thinking about us. Yet, we don't spend much time thinking about them. Think about that! So if you're ready to finally adjust your attitude and way of thinking, let's move forward.

Remember, how you think determines how you act; and how you act determines your results.

## THOUGHTS + ACTIONS = RESULTS

*Do you know why rats are smarter than humans? Drop a rat into a maze with 5 tunnels and place a piece of cheese at the end of the third tunnel. The rat will run down Tunnel 1 and find nothing there. Then he'll check out Tunnel 2 to again, find nothing. He'll then hit Tunnel 3 and find the cheese. Every time, thereafter, when you drop him in the maze, he'll head for Tunnel 3, because that's where the cheese is. If you move the cheese to Tunnel 4, he'll head down Tunnel 3, find no*

*cheese, probably hit Tunnel 2, still no cheese, then
check out Tunnel 4, find the cheese and be happy.
Conversely, a human will continue to go down
Tunnel 3 because that's the "right tunnel."*

We have been programmed all our lives regarding
the "right" way to think, to live, to act. Re-evaluating
that paradigm is vital to your moving forward.

*Our choicest plans have fallen
through,*

*Our airiest castles tumbled over,*

*Because of lines we neatly drew*

*And later neatly stumbled over.*

*–GROOKS*

How many habits and practices in your life do you
continue because they are the "right" or "comfortable" thing to do? When was the last time you took a
close, honest look, and evaluated if there is "cheese"
- a true reason/meaning for doing what you continue to do, even though you don't feel any progression
or movement forward in your life? Do the things

you do automatically, without even thinking, bring joy to your life? Have they contributed positively to your life or your path to success? What statements about yourself determine your actions? When did you last re-evaluate those definitives?

*"I don't like theatre."*
When is the last time you attended a play?

*"I don't like getting dressed up; these jeans are fine."*
When is the last time you got dressed up and per-haps experienced that you were treated differently?

*"I never meet anyone I could be interested in."*
When is the last time you changed where you hang out in order to meet different people?

*"I can't get a job that pays me more than I am making now."*
When was the last time you applied for a job that pays you more?

Here's our point: you're convinced that you won't succeed, so you don't even try. But by not trying, you've already failed.

> ***"Whether you think you can or you can't,***
> ***you are probably right."***
> \- Henry Ford

Changing your attitude from "I'm not good enough," to "I am a bright, motivated and successful person" will actually *empower* you to move forward. You'll experience a different feeling about yourself, and those around you also will experience this 'new' you.

Let me tell you a story about Zenna L., a college student:

*"I used to work for a company that was ready to hire me for a better position than I had. This caused me a lot of stress because not only would I be accepting more responsibilities in the position, but also, more stress. I didn't take the position, because I didn't feel ready for all those responsibilities. I also had the fear of success, which I regret."*

Zenna went on to explain: *"... people may fear the unknown, rather than taking up the challenge. They may prefer to stay in the situation they have because they're comfortable in it. But it's your choice to step up to the plate or to stay where you are. I think many people are afraid of taking a risk, because they are afraid of failing or even of becoming a success."*

An *"I-am-good-and-I-can-do-this"* attitude goes a long way.

Step 2:

# Find Your Way

## A. The 3 Stages of Life: Survival, Success, Significance

Our experience over the years is that there are three potential stages in a person's financial life: Survival, Success and Significance. Most people live in survival, or as Bob Proctor, Rhonda Byrne, and Wallace Wattles from <u>The Secret of Getting Rich</u> call it, *bondage.* This is your comfort zone; the place about which you don't have to think very much. You just go through life accepting what you have as "this is it." In this Survival Stage, you basically live paycheck to paycheck; working for someone else. Getting laid off or missing a few paychecks would cause financial turmoil in your life. You are at the mercy of what's going on in your life; or more importantly, you're not in charge or control of your life.

Getting out of the Survival Stage and into the Success and Significance Stages is discussed from here on out within this book, but don't expect a line-by-line manual on how to do it. Moving from one stage to the next is a journey – your journey. It starts with you and ends with you. Rediscovering yourself can be perhaps, the most fun, most exhilarating time of your life. But you have to grasp it, pursue it, and nurture it. Enough said. Let's continue.

The courageous people who get out of their way go on to experience Success and probably Significance. These stages allow you to enjoy the fruits of your labors, and the luxury of doing the things you want to do; as opposed to doing what you have to do, or are expected to do.

The Success Stage means that money is no longer a day-to-day issue for you. You have enough. Money, by the way, is like sex in a relationship: if you have enough, it's about 10% of the relationship. You rarely think about it; it's just there, part of the relationship. If you don't have enough, it becomes about 90% of the relationship. You think about it almost all the time. Whether or not you care about having wealth, money allows you **freedom** and **options**, both of which can contribute to your happiness.

When you master the art of getting out of your way *and staying out of your way*, then you have the opportunity to enter the Significance Stage of your life. This is where you can do incredible things for others by helping them to achieve the same Success and Significance Stages in their lives.

The Significance Stage is where the deep joy and satisfaction in life exist. Most people live their life believing that there is always some shortage of money, love, and success. I know there is plenty of all of those things to go around: plenty for anyone who commits to achieving them.

Throughout our years together, both of us have always been committed to giving *back*. The **time** and **skills** you donate are invaluable. And some giving requires cash. One of our current commitments involves sponsoring children who live in the radioactive fallout areas of the Chernobyl disaster for a medical respite in our country. You see, researchers have determined that if they can get them out of those areas which are still very toxic, for a minimum of 6 weeks a year, from the time they are seven years old, they can increase their life expectancies from 25 to 65 years. Our Belarusian 'daughter,' Karyna, has been coming to live with us during the summers for the past three years. It is pure joy to watch her health improve.

## B. Explore Your Goals, Dreams and Values

Take a good look at who you are, where you are, and where you want to go. Ask yourself these questions; and remember, be honest - the answers are only for your eyes.

Who are you? Describe yourself in 25 words or less. What is your style, your personality? What are your talents? Are you living your life by your parents' or someone else's rules? Are these paradigms controlling you? Is it your way or no way? Or are you too easily persuaded? Where are you now? Are you going in the right direction or are you off course for what you want to do in life?

What do you do now to make money? How do you relax? How do you create joy in your life and in the lives of others? What would you like to be doing that you are not yet doing? What would you like to know how to do?

What would you like to *stop* doing? What is the path that would accomplish your goals?

**Is your success a priority?**

These are all tough questions that I want you to contemplate as you continue with your re-evaluation of yourself.

I'd like you to write down the following:

What has stopped you from moving out of the Survival Stage?

_____

_____

What are your Goals (desires, ambitions, dreams):

    1. Short-Term [attainable in 1 year or less]

_____

_____

2. Long-Term [within 1-3 years and possibly 3-5 years]

_____

_____

_____

_____

What has stopped you from achieving your goals?

_____

_____

What priorities have you placed ahead of your goals?

_____

_____

Why?_____

If you blame other people or circumstances for where you are and don't want to be, then you're exactly where you belong. Many people have experienced the same type of circumstances, tragedies, bad luck, and worse, and have still achieved outrageous success. Don't waste your time or energy blaming other people for where you are right now. Be honest with yourself: the only person stopping you is YOU.

Maybe you're afraid, lack the experience, knowledge or skills to move forward; maybe you're a procrastinator; or maybe you're just plain lazy. Whatever it is, accept the responsibility. Acknowledge it, admit it and, once and for all, decide to do something about it. When you do, you will begin to find the joy in your life again. You will begin your journey into the next stage of your life. Let me tell you from experience, we are already there and would love for you to join us.

Larry and I are always telling folks, *"**Understanding** is the booby prize."* This means: Who cares *why* you are the way you are. What matters is that you acknowledge and accept who and what you are, and if it's in the way of your moving forward, figure out what to *do about it*.

**Larry SHARES:**
*Shirley was a waitress at a lovely San Jose restaurant who wanted to lose weight. One afternoon while she was serving me lunch, we chatted about what she was doing and where she wanted to go in life. Every time she brought another course she gave me another excuse why she couldn't do what she really wanted to do and why she couldn't lose weight. At the end of the evening, after I had suggested that none of what she was telling me was a valid reason for why she couldn't lose weight,*

*she gave me my check with a note on top of it. The note simply said, "I'm lazy."*

*Before I left, I made one more suggestion. I told her to put a list on her refrigerator of all the things she told me were in the way of her losing weight; and, therefore, every time she went to the refrigerator she would be reminded that SHE was in control. She smiled and came back to the table and showed me part of the list she had started putting together.*

The point of this story? Well, isn't it obvious? Identifying and acknowledging the circumstances you are blaming for your situation, and your complicity in that breakdown is actually a very *enlightening* discovery. It frees you to move toward solutions and pathways that have probably always been available. You were just too stuck on blaming others for your situation to see those opportunities. Let the **blame** go and experience how much lighter and freer you feel. Experience the excitement of assessing the opportunities available and moving toward positive rewards. Remember, you are not blaming yourself: blame has such heavy connotations and can be debilitating; it sticks you right where you are. Just simply acknowledge your responsibility and feel that knot in your chest go away.

A word about commiserating. We all know misery loves company, but whining with a co-worker about job dissatisfaction accomplishes only two things:

you feel worse as someone else reinforces how bad things are, and you remain firmly stuck there with that agreement. **Talk only to the person who can "forward the action" in a situation.** Your co-worker cannot do anything about the problem: talk to the supervisor with suggestions for improvement or solutions. In any aspect of business or personal communication, *talk only to the person who can forward the action.*

This little bit of advice will serve you well and keep you out of lots of troubles in your life.

In order to progress, you must realize that *you* are in your way.

Don't beat yourself up: just acknowledge what **is**. It doesn't make you a bad person: it makes you *human*.

**Larry SHARES:**

*I was coaching a woman who was going through some tough times; and at the end of one of our sessions she said, "I quit, I quit, I quit." The following day I saw her, and she said that she thought about what she had said and what I had told her about her being the constant when things didn't work out. She said that she cried all night and realized that she "always quit." That was her modus operandi. And it wasn't contributing at all to her life and the life she envisioned. She brought a hammer, tape measure and paint brush to our next meeting because she decided to "build a new life." She was going to carry her hammer, tape measure and paint brush with her in her purse so that whenever she had the urge to quit, she would be reminded that she had the power to not quit. She said she is known to live in her cave. She would stay in her house like a hermit, letting little from the outside world influence her. She looked me straight in the eye and said, "I am coming out of my cave, I'm getting out of my own way and not quitting again."*

Whether you are a Republican, Democrat or apolitical, regardless of how you voted, you must acknowledge that President Barack Obama was certainly raised with circumstances that could have been excellent and "valid" excuses for his achieving no success in the world. Yet he has achieved a lofty goal without allowing those circumstances to dictate his results. Remember:

**Thoughts (determine) + Actions (which produce) = Results**

What if his *mindset* had been *"Look how bad my childhood circumstances have been? I'll never get anywhere with this background."* Instead, it seems he must have believed, *"Look at my unconventional life: I must be headed for tremendous success."* Or perhaps, *"Wow, this life looks like a mess: this is not what I envision for my future. I will find the path out of here."* We don't know President Obama's thinking - he *never* calls - but it's clear he didn't spend much energy blaming unfortunate circumstances in his life, or using those situations as his excuse for failure. Whether you support the man or not doesn't matter: we are just using his visible situation as an example.

What excuses are you embracing that are paralyzing your growth? Be brutally honest with yourself.

## C. Defining and Controlling Your Timeline

We know. We're repeating ourselves; but it's worth repeating, over and over and over again: to get *out of* your way you have to realize that you are *in* your way. Analyze what you do on a daily basis. One of the first things you may tell yourself is that you don't have enough time to do the things you want to do. Well, we have news for you. Everyone has the same amount of time: 168 hours in the week, and that's it. But remember, it's what you do with that time that counts.

Here's an exercise to prove that you do have time that can be better utilized.

Keep a log and record what you do every 15 minutes for two days straight. Carry a small pad and pencil with you all the time. I know that is tough when performing some routine tasks, however, trust me, it is the only way you won't forget things.

Then, identify the things you've done that are not productive. Don't wait until the end of the day to fill this out – trust us, you will forget some of what you did during the day.

Now, think about what can be delegated to others or better yet, what can be eliminated from your daily routine. Make some tough decisions and you'll find an incredible amount of productive time just waiting for you to utilize.

And don't do this exercise just once. Periodically, throughout the year, complete this exercise. We have and we do; and recently we identified one of our biggest time thieves – EMAIL! This alerted us to the conclusion that many of us spend time on mundane tasks like email, because they are comfortable and allow us to put off all those "other" tasks we don't want to or feel like doing.

In truth, most of us have pretty full schedules most of the time. Many of us use lack of time as a primary excuse for not doing something we are avoiding. In Secrets of Question Based Selling, Thomas A. Freese offers a clever way to evaluate this game you play with yourself. To paraphrase his challenge: I have a magic wand, and I am going to wave it over your head. For the next week, every phone call you make will result in cash in your pocket. How many calls will you make? Hundreds? Thousands? You'll be in the bathroom with your cell phone on your coffee break, "smilin' and dialin!" If you make the task a priority, you will appropriate the time to get it done.

Take a good look at what you're **avoiding**: you'll find there is something unclear or something you don't understand about that task. Focus on that individual piece, clear it up, and you'll find that you're willing, relieved (and often actually excited) to cross it off your list, moving toward your next task/goal.

Finish what you're doing before you start something else. We live in a world of "multi-taskers." In fact, we even brag about how many tasks we can do concurrently. What we don't brag about is how effective we are; probably because we're not very effective at multi-tasking! We often settle for "that's good enough," and it rarely is.

## D. Adopting A Millionaire Mentality

We have asked people what they would do with unlimited Time, Money, Talent and Support. They understandably struggled with this question because it's something they never let themselves think about, because they don't have unlimited *anything*. We know there's no such thing; however, think about it anyway. You'll start identifying some of your dreams that may *not* be out of reach if you get out of the way of your getting them.

Think about changing your thinking from:

**HAVE + DO = BE** to **BE = DO + HAVE**

What in the world does that mean? Most of us think:

I must **HAVE** what millionaires have in order to **DO** what they do, and then, I will **BE** a millionaire.

Actually, that thinking is backwards. Instead, you must believe:

You are **(BE)** a millionaire. (I don't care if your money is not yet on deposit; we're talking about changing the way you *think,* remember?) And you can **DO** what millionaires do (or whatever else you *want* to do). Then you can **HAVE** what millionaires have (or whatever else you want to have).

Can you see that you shift from being "at the effect" to being in charge, just by altering your mindset?

We know this concept may be tricky, so let us elaborate. Change your attitude from a wannabe to "I am." When you come from BEING (acknowledging yourself as a bright, capable, powerful person), you can actually DO and HAVE whatever you want. Warren Buffet, one of the richest men in America, doesn't live in a fancy house. He still lives in a very modest, three-bedroom home in the town where he grew up. Ever notice how very wealthy people often dress indifferently? It's because they can dress any way they want. They already come from "BEING."

Their "DO" and "HAVE" rules are totally at their discretion.

### MARILYN SHARES:

*Years ago, I worked as Press Secretary for a very wealthy U.S. Congressman. His shoes were very fine shoes, but they always had holes in the soles. His very elegant topcoat sported a silk lining in tatters. In fact, when he visited the White House for dinner one night, and the butler graciously took his coat, correctly turning it inside out and folding it over his arm, the Congressman was both surprised and mortified to observe the tattered lining on display for all to see. He had simply never noticed or cared about it.*

Who can modify your mindset? YOU. Think as though you *are* where you want to *be*: think "I Am." Many sports coaches utilize this type mindset in teaching athletic skills. They insist their students "visualize" themselves executing the perfect golf swing/tennis slam/swan dive. They believe that unless you can visualize it, you won't ever be able to actually accomplish it.

Successful people don't let their *"I can't afford it"* thinking get in their way. *"I can't afford it"* is the lazy man's way of thinking. Your brain shuts down: *"Oh, I can't afford it. Oh well... "* (and you will have just scored another lost opportunity. What did it cost you?)

Whether you're talking about **time** or **money**, shift your thinking to *"HOW can I afford it?"* That is the Millionaire Mentality. Your brain gets busy on a **solution**: *"What do I need? A partner, a lender, creative strategies, what?"*

Look at the **potential** of opportunities and not the **cost**. How many times have you seen a vacant lot and/or building and said to yourself, *"Someone is going to do something very exciting with that property and they are going to make a lot of money."*

Who are **they**? Why don't *you* become *they*? You're literally giving away the opportunity to someone else.

**LARRY SHARES:**

*If I told you I had a beautiful briefcase that I wanted to sell for $10,000, you'd probably think I was crazy: the **cost** is way too high. You'd want nothing to do with it. But, what if I told you the briefcase had $25,000 cash inside? Then would you be interested in buying it from me? Of course you would. In fact, you'd buy it even if you didn't have the money. You'd find the money, because you'd clearly see the **potential**. Not having the money in your bank account would not stop you: you'd find a way to do it. We often get stuck using **cost** (time or money) as our excuse for not acting. By focusing, instead, on **potential**, we get **out of our own way** and find ourselves **on our way** to a solution and greater success.*

Whether it's *time* or *money*, evaluate first the **potential of an opportunity.**

That is the "MM" - the MILLIONAIRE MENTALITY. Don't get in your way of opportunities just because you can't always see the specific and definitive path to the results you want. You don't need to see the path; you just need to have and hold the vision of what you want. The clearer the vision, the better your chance of achieving it. Think about that for a moment. If you don't have a clear picture of your desire, how in the world will you know when it shows up?

Step 3:
# Be On Your Way

## A. Fight the Fear

*Here is a fact that should help you fight a bit longer:*

*Things that don't actually kill you outright make you stronger.*

*–GROOKS*

What is the number one cause of your current paralysis? Fear. Your fear is what stops you from taking advantage of opportunities. An opportunity presents itself and automatically you go into an *"analysis paralysis"* stage. stage. You overthink, vividly imagining every terrible possibility. Not surprisingly, you scare yourself to death, which stops you in your tracks.

Marie Curie once said:

*"Nothing in life is to be feared. It is only to be understood."*

### LARRY SHARES:

*One of my mentors told me that "fear is the dark room where negatives are developed." Think about that and interpret it as you see it. Perhaps your fears keep you from entering a dark room (unknown); or perhaps the dark room is the state in which you put yourself where negative emotions develop. Your fear will keep you from entering that dark room; however, only by entering into the room can a beautiful picture be developed. Just think about all the things you have feared and yet never experienced. What a waste of emotion and energy - energy you could have utilized to fuel your journey to success.*

*When I was little I was sure that the Bogeyman was lurking in the basement and I would never go there alone. I knew, however, that a shelf in the basement was where my Mom kept candy. By not going down there, I was literally depriving myself of the "goodies." Finally one day, my desire for candy outweighed my fear. I cautiously opened the door and crept down the stairs. I got the goodies! And sweeter than the taste of that candy was the personal elation I felt about conquering my fear of that room. I've never forgotten that feeling and how "proud of myself" I felt.*

*(The candy was pretty good, too.) The next time fear slowed my progress, I remembered how good it felt to overcome that fear. It motivated me.*

*Now, haven't you experienced something similar? All that energy that I put into fearing something I had not experienced could have been used in a much more productive way.*

Let's put a specific face on your barriers. Take a few minutes to list some of the fears that have gotten in the way of your accomplishing your plans and dreams:

_____

_____

_____

_____

I'd bet that you haven't experienced many of these. You've probably been told on numerous occasions that *"This isn't for you," "It'll never work," "You can't succeed in this endeavor,"* and/or *"You'll just get hurt."* Ever notice that critics know the *cost* of everything and the *value* of nothing?

So first, remember, evaluate the *potential*. If the potential for success is there, then go to the next step: acknowledge your "feelings" about the opportunity.

Write this down and put it where you will see it every day:

**FEAR:**

    False

    Evidence

    Appearing

    Real

We understand that if you have a pulse, you have some amount of fear; however, there is **good** fear and **bad** fear. Good, rational fear is, for example: *"If I walk into the middle of the highway at rush hour, I'm afraid I'll get hit by a car and get hurt."* Good thinking - this is the type of rational fear that keeps us alive.

The bad or crippling fear is that little voice in your head that says over and over again: *"Well, what IF...?"* You've probably what-iffed yourself back into the same familiar and suffocating traps your entire life.

During our national training workshops, we always discuss fear. We ask our students what their biggest fears are. Interestingly, the top two fears are almost always FAILURE and SUCCESS - *equally*. How can that be? Think about it. What is the common denominator? They are both *unknowns*. The unknown is what creates discomfort and resistance. It's no different than your first day, as a youngster, at a new school, for instance. You're probably not afraid of getting physically hurt – you're simply uncomfortable because you don't know if:

- the teacher will be nice;
- the other kids will like you;
- you'll like the other kids;
- your desk will be where you want it;
- the work will be too hard.

Another huge fear many people have is of losing money. How much money have you already lost by not taking action and by letting opportunities pass you by? You then see others profit from the opportunities you let get away and you want to kick yourself. You've probably even told yourself that NEXT TIME you're going to take advantage of that opportunity. But, when another opportunity does come by, your fears once again hold you back.

Isn't it time to get over your fears and turn that energy into something more productive?

**MARILYN SHARES:**
*Years ago, my adorable stepdaughter, Jodi, came to me and said she had decided to run for high school class secretary. Naturally, I said, "Great." With a huge, teenage rolling of the eyes, she sighed, "I have to give a speech." Again, I said, "Great." She elaborated, assuming I obviously had not grasped the enormity of this fact, "...in front of the entire school, in an assembly." Still*

*I said, "Wow, that's great." Another sigh as she reluctantly pointed out, "I'm scared."*

*I acted confused: "Scared? Of making a speech?" "Yes." (Eye roll: I mean, how could I be so dense?) I probed, "What do you mean scared?" "Afraid." (How dumb was I, anyway?)*

*I then asked, "Well, what does that feel like - physically, I mean?" "Well," she pondered, "my hands are damp and cold, my mouth is really dry, my knees are a little shaky, and my stomach feels very bad."*

*"Oh," I said happily: "you're EXCITED.""I am?" Jodi asked in wonder. "Yeah," I assured her, "shaky knees, dry mouth, wet hands, bad stomach - that's excited all right." "Oh," she said, somewhat mollified. "Well, would you help me with the speech?" "Sure," I said, thrilled.*

*So we crafted a speech, Jodi rehearsed well, and she delivered a fabulous speech (yes, we got permission to sneak into the balcony at school to watch)! She went on to win the election and, as importantly, continued in leadership roles in college.*

*Six years later, Jodi was graduated from college and began working at our advertising agency. She was assisting me on a big, industrial account and we were running a huge convention for the client in New Orleans: 3000 hotel rooms, trade show floor, agenda, session schedules, etc. The day Larry and I were scheduled to leave for New Orleans to run the convention, we both came down with the worst flu either of us has ever had: knee-walking, commode-hugging, you-are-not-going-anywhere flu. Jodi was the only other person with any knowledge of the account or client.*

*We called her and said, "You have to fly to New Orleans today and run this convention." She immediately started giving us all the reasons why she couldn't do it. She was talking so fast coming up with a litany of negatives that it was hard to understand her. After some parental and professional (after all she did work for the agency) coaxing she came over and sat at the foot of our bed taking copious notes while we briefed her on everything we could think of. Finally, it was time to pack up and fly to New Orleans.*

*I said, "Okay, you're ready to go. How are you?" Jodi paused and nervously responded, "I think I'm really EXCITED." We laugh about that lesson to this day.*

You can turn your fears into excitement: just rename those physical sensations---the stomach, the shaky knees, sweaty palms. That's for sure *excitement*. Let the unknown *energize* you rather than *stifle* you. It's totally in your power to reposition how you view those feelings. Identify your fears. Rename them. Embrace them. Your fears don't have to disappear;

it's actually okay to have those emotional feelings and still act rationally. In the example above, we renamed Jodi's fear of speaking in front of a group in order to "unplug" her automatic mindset from being "afraid" to "excited." She was then able to plan her actions without the influence of feeling afraid. Remember, most of the time, the scenarios we imagine are far worse than anything that has ever happened to us, which is what creates our barriers.

*As Mark Twain noted, "I been afraid of many things in my life...some of which actually happened?"*

There are two factors that will help you overcome your fears.

## KNOWLEDGE and EXPERIENCE

Let's talk about **knowledge** and how to achieve it. Inform yourself; do your homework; and surround yourself with successful people who support you and are good at the things that you may not be. You don't have to be the best at everything. As Wallace Wattles tells us in <u>The Secret Science of Getting Rich</u>, the *Law of Relativity* is always in effect. This law states that everything is relative to the position that you are in and it depends on how you look at things. Use *The Law* against yourself, and you'll always think people are better than you. Use *The Law* in your favor, and you'll always be able to do something better than someone else. In other words, instead of focusing on what you cannot bring to the party, focus instead on that at which you excel. Remind yourself and let your co-workers know, "I'm all over this task---very comfortable handling it. Can one of you address this second part?" Then observe how someone else handles something at which you have no confidence or even skill. You are gaining **knowledge.**

The second factor that will catapult you past your fears is **experience.**

Experience is something you have to earn yourself. If you never let yourself experience what you're afraid of, you'll never gain experience, which in turn creates **confidence**.

Write this down:

### Knowledge + Experience = Confidence

Eleanor Roosevelt, one of the greatest and highest profile women in American history, was asked what made her such a strong woman. She replied, *"I do something that scares me every day."*

What "scares" you and prevents you from doing what you know you should be doing? Face your fears; don't run from them. Acknowledge your feelings, embrace them and act anyway. Having fear and acting anyway is one of the most exhilarating and powerful feelings you'll ever experience. Might you fail sometimes? I certainly expect so: if you never fail, you're probably not trying hard enough.

Will Rogers offered this opinion: "Good judgment comes from experience, and a lot of that comes from bad judgment."

Ask yourself if it's okay to have your "fears" and do what you need to do anyway. Is it okay with you to learn from experience? Make sure your answer is a resounding YES. If you never experience anything new, you'll probably never learn anything new.

### LARRY SHARES:

*Marilyn and I are downhill skiers and enjoy skiing out West in the spring. Years ago, we were skiing in Aspen, and Marilyn turned to me and observed: "You know, we are skiing HALF the mountain." For those of you who don't ski, let me explain: Ski slopes are marked with round green signs (easiest slopes); blue square signs (intermediate); black diamonds (advanced skill required); and double black diamonds (are you CRAZY?). We were happily skiing the green and the blue slopes. We'd pass a black diamond or double black diamond, look the other way, and move on to another green or blue. Marilyn said, "This is stupid. Let's get some instruction to move us to the level where we can enjoy skiing the entire mountain."*

*So we hired an instructor to ski with us all day and finely tune our skills. At the end of the day, he said, "Okay, you're good to go." "Well," we asked, "what can we ski?" "You can ski the mountain," he answered. "Well, I mean, can we* ski the black diamonds?" "Yeah," he assured us. "How about the double blacks?" "Yeah, you can ski the mountain." So off we went, as fast as we could, to the first double black we encountered. It was called "Shock." (Funny, how you remember things like that.) We enthusiastically skied up to the edge and observed the slope. Wow. It was really steep, really narrow, and really long, and had lots of moguls (bumps). We studied it carefully for a few minutes, then side-stepped up the slope about 10 feet. "Okay," Marilyn said. "We can ski this." "Yup," I agreed. "Okay, 'let's do it."

Neither one of us moved. "You first." We thought a few minutes more, then side-stepped back down to the edge. Can you believe that the slope had gotten narrower, steeper, longer, and bumpier in just those few minutes? Back up the slope we went and regarded each other. "If I look down that slope again," Marilyn confessed, "I will never ski it. We have the skill (knowledge); we just don't have the experience, yet. Let's just DO IT. TOGETHER, at the same time. And if you cheat, I will kill you." We agreed. We stayed away from the edge, and on the count of three, we both skied the slope. By the time we reached the bottom, we both had our poles in the air, and we were both screaming for joy and jubilation. It was one of the most stimulating and enlightening experiences in our lives.

To acknowledge that kind of fear, embrace it, and

*act anyway was one of the most powerful acts we
have ever enjoyed. To this day, when a fear bar-
rier arises, we will periodically remind each other
to "just ski the slope."*

**Will ya? Won't ya? Aren't you gonna?
If I let you won't ya wanna?
Aw, come on you said you could;
Whatsa' matter? Are you scared?**

- Anonymous

## B. Creative Visualization

Here are six easy things you can do to help you stay
out of your way:

- Think creatively (outside the box);
- Increase your awareness of everything
  around you;
- Associate with successful people;
- Raise the level of your circle of friends and
  associates;
- Take advantage of opportunities; and
- Follow your instincts.

### LARRY SHARES:

*I went to college wanting to be a lawyer. I took
all the right classes, joined all the right clubs
and was even elected an officer of my freshman
class. Then I was asked to become the business
manager for our college newspaper. I found my-*

*self writing very nice sized commission checks to the advertising manager, while I received a smaller fixed tuition grant for college. So I did the only logical thing and demoted myself, hired a business manager and took over the advertising manager position. It wasn't long before I realized that it was a career in advertising that I wanted as opposed to becoming a lawyer.*

*After college graduation, I spent over a year interviewing and finally had a company offer me a position with a draw against future commission. In other words, I would owe them money and had to pay it back out of my future commissions. This didn't feel good to me, so I told them to let me work for them with no pay at all; and when I started making money for them, they could start paying me what I was worth to them. Two years later, I was asked to be a partner in the company.*

*You see, what I had not realized at that time, was that I had already envisioned myself as a success. In my mind I was already there. I had supreme confidence in myself; and all I had to do was do more than what was expected of me every day and let the vision happen.*

The point is that I didn't understand how it was going to happen - only that it would - and it did. We don't have to know the exact path we are going to take to attain our desires. What I've learned is that we have to start living our dreams, our positive thoughts, feelings and actions - and our dreams and desires will appear.

**LARRY CONTINUES:**

*Sometimes, when I got on a downslide, I slid hard and fast, because I was concentrating on my problems. It's like going down a slide in a playground. It is much harder to control your slide when you wax that slide. Consistent negative thoughts are like waxing your slide in the wrong direction. I was literally getting in my own way, faster and faster, of achieving positive things because I was only thinking how bad things were. I was in my own way.*

Finding your way may come through activities that you didn't expect. Remember, an extracurricular activity led to my advertising career.

A person I studied under said to me that communication equals wealth. Talk to people about your goals and dreams. Learn how to speak effectively, communicating your thoughts in a persuasive, confident manner. If you don't project confidence in your own ideas, if you don't get excited, then you won't excite anyone else.

Recite this little "Grook" to yourself:

*Sun that givest all things birth,*
*Shine on everything on earth!*
*If that's too much to demand,*
*Shine at least on this our land.*
*If even that's too much for thee,*
*Shine at any rate on me.*

*—GROOKS*

## C. Heighten Your Awareness

It is totally okay to focus on your own success. When you reach Success you are on your way to Significance. **Make no mistake, Success is a wonderful, comfortable place to be.** My experience is that once people have enjoyed that tranquility for a while, they feel the need to reach out and do more... achieve a level where they can make a difference for others. When you arrive at Significance, you are now at the place when you contribute to the lives of others. What a wonderful, joyful place to be.

Recognize *opportunities*. They usually come disguised as *challenges*. Be prepared to gratefully accept challenges because they may lead you to the places you've been seeking.

Turn your interest or involvement into commitment.

Do you know the difference between involvement and commitment? When you look at a plate of bacon and eggs, you know the chicken was *involved:* the pig was *committed.*

Be thoughtful about restricting yourself when setting goals and making action plans. Do you really need to set those parameters, or might you be willing to just follow a path and see where it leads, without specific expectations?

*As Pastor X steps out of bed,*
*He slips a neat disguise on:*
*The halo 'round his priestly head*
*Is really his horizon.*

*—GROOKS*

Where have you set your horizons?

Be committed to what it takes. Ken Blanchard said, *"There is a difference between being interested and being committed. If you're interested, you'll do it if it's convenient. If you're committed, you'll do whatever it takes."* Chicken or pig?

General interest doesn't get it done - **commitment ensures success.** If you are not committed to your future success, find a comfy chair and pick a liquor. At this point, it's important to write down things you're committed to achieving. Create a **Commitment Card** and keep it in your wallet.

---

**Get Out of Your Way**
*Commitments to Me.*

I absolutely commit myself to the following:

_____

_____

_____

_____

_____

Signature _____ Date _____

---

Your commitments will control your thoughts and in turn your perspective and actions. If the people with whom you surround yourself do not share your commitment, do what Bob Proctor from <u>The Secret of Getting Rich</u> says, *"Don't hang around them as often; and when you do, don't stay long."* I do love that.

I want you to picture your daily life as a big, straight-sided jar. Sitting beside this jar, you have two large rocks, which represent two priorities: 1) your mental and physical health and well being; and, 2) your financial future and security. You also have a pile of pebbles, which represents your family, your job, and perhaps your care of extended family. A pile of sand represents your hobbies, your social life, your leisure activities, and trips to the mall. Finally, a large pitcher of water represents your spirituality.

If you put the two big rocks in the jar first, there's plenty of room for the pebbles; they find empty space and fill it. The sand then pours perfectly into the cracks; and, finally, the water fills the jar to the top - *perfectly.*

If, however, you do NOT consciously put the two rocks into your jar first, guess what happens? The pebbles find their way into the jar first; the sand leaps in and guess what? There's NO ROOM for your two priorities: your mental and physical health and well being; and your financial future and security. You're the only person who can make these priorities - and you must do so every day. If you consciously do this exercise every day for three weeks, it will become a habit, and you will break your old habits in the process.

Now, I have to tell you that most people feel compelled to fill *your* jar with *their* priorities. Don't get me wrong. It's not that they're bad people - it's just human nature. You, however, are the ONLY one in charge of your jar. Be selfish. Be vigilant. This may be the first time in your life that you have been told it's okay to be selfish. And, allow yourself a few chuckles over our nature as human beings.

> I see and I hear
>    And I speak no evil:
> I carry no malice
>    within my breast:
> Yet quite without wishing
>    A man to the devil
> One may be permitted
>    to hope for the best.
>
> —GROOKS

Don't waste time trying to change people's minds. They will resist.

Wallace Wattles, in <u>The Secret of Getting Rich</u> said, *"People don't resist change, they resist being changed."* However, if you change how you do things, others will follow. If you emit positive vibrations, you will attract positives just as certain as negative people attract more negatives.

I'm sure you've experienced this. For example, when a positive person walks into a room they can lift the spirits of all the people in the room just as a negative person can bring everyone down. Haven't we all been those people at one time or another? Sure we have. I have a friend who creates stress wherever he goes. Things can be calm and peaceful and within 10 minutes of his arrival, chaos prevails. It got so bad that one day I asked him why he had so much stress. He told me he didn't have any stress at all – that he was just fine. I said, "If you don't have stress, then you must be a carrier." Some of us are indeed carriers of emotions. We can swing the mood of a room with no problem at all. Now that you're aware of this, try to always be a **carrier of positives** and notice the positive backwash you experience.

People like to be around positive people. Oh, some may enjoy commiserating about shared aggravations, but not for the long run. All that accomplishes is to make both of you feel worse. Eventually, they will move on to someone more fun to be around. Again, it's human nature.

If you're going to get out of your way, then you know that you have to change certain things in your life, and you also know that change can be hard. Someone once said, *"If you want to change some things in your life, you've got to change some things in your life."*

Let's do an exercise… and please be totally honest with yourself. I want you to mentally change five (5) things about your physical appearance right now. (In fairness to yourself, do not read the next paragraph until you are done with this exercise.) **Write down what you have envisioned changing.**

1.

2.

3.

4.

5.


Now, imagine changing 10 more things about your physical appearance. **Write these things down.**

1.

2.

3.

4.

5.

6.

7.

8.

9.

10.

Take a look at what you did. Did you remove things? Most people think they have to *lose* something when they change. That is why you probably started taking something off. Change should be looked at as a positive. What can you change about yourself to make you a more powerful, more positive, more effective person?

**LARRY SHARES:**

*I used to be a terrible nail biter. My parents tried everything they could think of to make me stop. I was constantly told to "take your fingers out of your mouth," which I did; only to find my fingers right back in my mouth moments later! My parents put terrible tasting stuff on my fingers, and after a while it didn't taste so bad. My nail biting was a terrible habit I didn't think I'd ever break. Then, one day, Marilyn asked me to go with her to run some errands; and when I asked her where we were going, she said to get a manicure. I immediately told her that I didn't need to sit there while she was getting a manicure. But then she told me that it wasn't for her, but for me. "I don't think so, MEN don't get manicures," I replied. So while I was sitting there getting a manicure, I started studying how my hands actually looked. Guess what? They looked pretty good even though there wasn't too much nail to work with the first time. In fact, I found myself admiring them frequently. I wanted them to continue to look nice, so I didn't want to put them back in my mouth. I eventually stopped biting my nails. I realized that it was a very positive change for me psychologically, which added greatly to my physical and perceptual appearance. I spent all those years biting my nails, feeling bad about it, (probably looking nervous and insecure!), and assuming I'd never be able to stop. I assumed it was just one of those habits I'd have in my life. Never did I think I could break it; but I guess I never committed to making that change. Once I did; it was obvious that I could, and I did. Sometimes, we need to remind ourselves that we can make a difference; we just have to want the change to occur.*

Think about how many things you've resisted even trying because you weren't sure you could succeed? Give yourself more credit than you are right now. Do things you're not sure you can do. You'll be surprised at the number of times you will enjoy success. Success is an empowering feeling. Start with something small. When you've succeeded at that, raise the bar. The greater the resistance; the greater the reward.

Take a minute to write down what we call our "elevator speech:" this is a brief (15 second) description of **what you do**. Make it positive and interesting enough to arrest the attention of the person to whom you are speaking...enough so that they will question you further. You have a lot to offer: start sharing it! Remember, what may be "old hat" to you might be fascinating new information to someone you've just met.

_____

_____

_____

_____

Step 4:

# Sidestep Outside Obstacles in Your Way

## A. Discipline and Commitment

You must be both **effective** and **efficient** during your journey.

Effectiveness is doing the right things. Efficiency is reflected in doing things the right way. Your activities must be in line with both; for if you did all the wrong things absolutely right (or the right things absolutely wrong) the result would be a perfect disaster.

Taking chances is part of life. If you're not willing to take risks, you won't get any goodies in return. If you're unwilling to chance a bump or two, you won't get any bennies. (Remember the candy in my basement??) That's life.

### LARRY & MARILYN SHARE:
*Life is actually very much like the game of Monopoly. There are two basic types of players, and how you play speaks volumes about how you approach life. There is the conservative player and the aggressive player. Each is given the same $1500 when the game begins. The conservative player, the one who hoards his money, takes no*

*risks and can't wait to go all around the board to pass "Go" because the bank then gives him more money; a salary, if you will. The conservative player lives in the Survival Stage.*

*During the first part of the game, he's very happy because his money keeps accumulating. The other player, the aggressive one, is taking advantage of opportunities and taking some chances; he's buying property, investing, and thus begins to have less and less cash. The conservative player has no cares since he has cash; however, what he doesn't realize is that he's not building any security for the future. Remember, just like in our world, you can't save yourself to wealth.*

*The aggressive player buys everything he lands on; even if he must mortgage properties do it. As the game progresses, the conservative player, or hoarder, begins to land on owned properties and must pay rent on a house, then on a hotel; ultimately, losing the game to the bold adventurer who "went for it" and played "full out," putting his future at risk, in order to achieve success.*

Playing full out requires *effort*. It does not require *struggle*.

If you go to the grocery store and buy groceries, you bring them home and put them away in the pantry and refrigerator. That required effort. It did not require struggle. Struggle is just effort with negative emotions attached - yes, your 'reasons' why you can't possibly do it, or don't want to do it! Struggle is created when YOU put negative energy on effort.

In this case, if you hated grocery shopping and spent hours or days agonizing over having to go, then that would require struggle, wouldn't it? Perhaps you even resist that task so much that you refused to learn where to locate the items you frequently purchase. In that case, you probably have created unnecessary stress when none was required.

*Problems worthy of attack*

*Prove their worth by hitting back.*

*—GROOKS*

You must Talk the Walk: communication brings wealth. Tell people what you're doing or want to do.

This commits you to doing it. Won't you be embarrassed when the people you told you were going to do something (a new venture) ask you about your business and you haven't done anything? The more people you tell about your intentions, the more likely you are to do it and succeed. The people you tell become your *motivators*. If you don't tell anyone, how many people will know? It's like winking at a person in the dark. You know what you're doing, but no one else does - how effective is that?

My dad taught me to always ask for the order:

> *"I want to do business with you;*
> *can we start tomorrow?"*

Think of how many times someone has tried to sell you something or change your mind to agree with him. He extols all the features and benefits of what he is selling and then stops and looks at you, waiting for you to say something and make up your mind. However, he never asked you directly to buy his services. He expected you to come to that conclusion yourself. How many "orders" or negotiations have you lost doing the same thing?

*Losing one glove is certainly painful,*

*but nothing compared to the pain*

*of losing one, throwing away the other*

*and finding the first one again*

*—GROOKS*

As my dad said, ***"If you never ask, the default answer is always no."*** When you don't ask for the order, you are getting in the way of people making a decision. You'll find that people respect you, your time, and your professionalism when you play full out and bring your conversations to a decision-making conclusion.

Continue to assist your colleague in identifying his concerns, objections, questions, reservations, or barriers, until you've responded to his reservations and cleared them up for him. Don't fear his objections; embrace them so he can articulate them and work rationally through them. This is how you bring him to "choice." This is how you get "yeses" in business and in life.

Get in the GAME: the GAME of GETTING RICH – of ACCUMULATING WEALTH. Take charge of your life.

- Some of you are LISTENERS: you've HEARD there's a game, but don't really understand it.

- Some of you are WATCHERS: you WATCH the game, but you're not in it.

- Some of you are CLUELESS: you're not even AWARE that there is a game.

You have to PLAY to WIN.

So, GET SUITED UP: focus on HOW you're getting in the game - which methods are you going to employ to get in the game?

Do you think it's important to have a coach and playbook? Even Tiger Woods has a coach and playbook.

STUDY YOUR PLAYBOOK: the 'rules of engagement' if you will. Review your HOME STUDY COURSES, listen to your coaches, and your mentors so you understand HOW to play. What methods will you utilize to make money? What will you do to bring more joy into your life? You do have choices. *Decide*.

*Whenever you're called on to make up your mind,*

*And you're hampered by not having any,*

*The best way to solve the dilemma, you'll find,*

*Is simply by spinning a penny.*

*No, not so that chance shall decide the affair
While you're passively standing there moping;*

*But the moment the penny is up in the air,*

*You suddenly know what you're hoping.*

*—GROOKS*

The previous Grook quote is true. Try it. We find most people who are stuck at a decision point are able to pretty fairly evaluate their choices. Their dilemma, however, is that they don't want to surrender *options*. Learn to let it go. You can always go back up the trail and take another path. **Just choose and go.**

Remember, millionaires have multiple sources of income; so you're not necessarily restricted to one choice. Start, however, by identifying a course(s) of action that is doable in your timeframe. If you overload yourself, you may become overwhelmed and paralyzed by your "to do" list.

PLAY. Don't just listen. PLAY. Don't just watch. You've been doing that your entire life, up until now. You're reading this now because you want to play - effectively and efficiently.

*The joy is in playing.*

Start enjoying yourself. Ask yourself:
- Do you have joy in your life?

- Do you bring joy into other peoples lives?

- Remember, **significance is the stage of life in which deep joy exists.** This is the stage of life where you recognize that time is worth much more than money. Wouldn't you rather live there?

**MARILYN SHARES:**
*When I am teaching a class of students who are desperate to make money...and I'm trying to get them to understand that **time** is more valuable than **money**...I employ this exercise: I select the youngest person in the room - usually someone around twenty or younger. I then say this:*

*"I have a deal for you: I will sign over to you all my assets - property, bank accounts...everything." (Their face alights with expectation.) "In exchange, I get to be your age again, and you must become **my** age." Since I am obviously many decades older than they, this stops them cold. They usually ponder, blush (being polite) and say, "No deal." Of course it's no deal: you can always make*

> *more money, but you cannot beg, borrow or steal*
> *more time. It is invaluable. I will tell you a funny*
> *story: once when I offered that deal to a young*
> *man and he turned it down, a 94-year-old stu-*
> *dent in the back of the room yelled out, "I'll take*
> *that deal!" The class collapsed in laughter.*

There are opportunities everywhere. If not these opportunities - those that appear today and tomorrow
- then what? If not today or tomorrow, then when?
When is a good time to get started on the rest of your
life? Are you willing to give yourself permission to
succeed?

Get out of your way right now and get on your way.
Ask yourself this:

***What would I do if I knew that whatever I do I***
***wouldn't fail?***

How aggressive would you be if you knew you
couldn't fail?

Put a jar or any type of container on your desk and
pretend there's a Genie in it that will grant you success in 100% of your endeavors. Whenever you tend
to get in your way of taking advantage of an opportunity we want you to remember the Genie. Obviously,
there isn't a real Genie; but, if you don't make calls,
if you don't recognize opportunities, if you let your
old beliefs, paradigms, habits (your old ways of doing things) get in your way, you won't experience the
success you want and you won't get past your fears.

Will you make mistakes? Probably. But remember, if you don't ever make a mistake, you're not trying hard enough. When you make an error, should you quit and go home? No.

*The road to wisdom? Well, it's plain and simple to express:*

> *Err*
>
> *And err*
>
> *And err, again;*
>
> *But less*
>
> *And less*
>
> *And less.*

*–GROOKS*

Most people set goals. We want you to set goals; and then we want you to create a specific action plan for achieving those goals. Actions plans are more definitive tasks that you can prioritize until they are accomplished. Plans outline the steps needed to achieve your goals. They form the stairway to your goals, one step at a time.

Again, in today's economy *it is impossible to save your way to wealth*. In about 1971, President Nixon took us off the gold standard. Since that time, with our dollars not being backed by actual gold, our dollar is being devalued. We must, therefore, recognize wealth-building opportunities and make money in myriad ways. Remember, we mentioned previously that most truly wealthy people have multiple streams of income. Some of these incomes come to them while they're sleeping and while they're doing other things. This is an excellent strategy to employ; and it will require you to step out of your comfort zone and accept challenges and opportunities *when they arise.*

**Each opportunity knocks only once. If you don't answer the door, someone else will.**

Be on your way with confidence.

Address issues as they arise, one at a time. And remember, every victory makes you stronger.

Eric Hoffer said it very well and put confidence into a practical perspective. He said, *"To learn you need a certain degree of confidence, not too much and not too little. If you have too little confidence, you will think you can't learn. If you have too much, you will think you don't have to learn."*

At a 1970 Human Resources conference, which was my major in college, a speaker said, *"In times of change the learners will inherit the earth, while the learned find themselves beautifully equipped to deal with a world that no longer exists."*

The past---well, it's just like
   Our dear Great-Aunt Laura
        Who cannot or will not per-
ceive
That though she is welcome,
   And though we adore her,
      Yet, now, it is time to leave.
                    *–GROOKS*

Knowledge and the confidence to use the knowledge we acquire will keep us from getting in our way. Don't let "what-iffing" immobilize you.

> *Problems worthy of attack*
> *Prove their worth by hitting back.*
>                    *—GROOKS*

## B. Creating A Task Table

> *Put in a place*
> *Where it's easy to see*
> *The cryptic admonishment*
>            *T.T.T.*
> *When you feel how depressingly*
> *Slowly you climb,*
> *It's well to remember that*
>   *Things Take Time.*
>                    *—GROOKS*

**This is where you write the rest of this book and keep it with you as a working document. It will keep you out of your way.**

Write down your burning desires that you have put off because you have gotten in your way.

Set a **task table** for yourself and remember these are your tasks so you and you alone can change them.

I am on my way to_____
(Wealth)

I am on my way to_____
(Health)

I am on my way to_____
(Family)

I am on my way to _____
(Joy)

I am on my way to _____
(Satisfaction)

Say out loud, *"I'm ON MY WAY."* Say it again only louder this time.

*"I AM ON MY WAY!"*

Remember, *life is a journey, not a destination.*

Enjoy the journey and know the destination. Remember, without a destination how will you know if you get there? Imagine yourself flying on a mystery trip from Buffalo (we know you are probably asking why Buffalo? Because that's where we live) and the pilot says his friendly *"Thank you for flying with us,"* and when you ask him where you're going, he says, *"I don't know."*

Without a destination what do you think will happen after he flies around for several hours trying to decide? That's right, you'll run out of fuel and crash and burn. We don't want you to run out of fuel and crash and burn.

**It bears repeating: If you don't know where you're going, how will you know when you get there?**

Have a clear picture in your mind of what you want; visualize it down to the smallest detail. Commit yourself to its realization and make it part of your everyday life. Then enjoy it when it appears.

Living is a thing you do

now or never - which do you?

*–GROOKS*

## C. Prioritizing Tasks

Will you fall back into your comfort zone when things get challenging and your to-do list is longer than you care to address?

When Bob Proctor asked Earl Nightingale, *"How do you manage your time to fit in all you do?"* He answered, "No one can manage time," but went on to explain that he focuses on *activities*, giving everything he has to each activity until it's complete. He then moves on to the next one.

This is in direct contrast to the way most of us work in this age of technology. Remember, as we said earlier, the buzzword for our generation is multitasking, and we're proud of it. The more we can do, simultaneously, the prouder we are; we even brag about it.

We suggest revisiting this philosophy and get more into **task managing**. By doing this, our effectiveness has increased along with our individual efficiency. What a feeling of accomplishment you'll get when you look back and observe that all those tasks on your list are **completed** and not just partially done.

### MARILYN SHARES:

*We have two framed needlepoints my mother stitched for us that help keep us on track. One says, "If you don't have time to do it right, when will you ever have time to do it over?"*

Write this down: **"Good enough is not good enough."** Take the time to do it right and completely the first time.

Don't revert back to old habits.

Do more than you're required to do for each task. One of the big secrets to getting ahead is not letting your old habits (like "that's good enough") get in your way. Always do more than your job or assignment requires.

### MARILYN CONTINUES:

*The other needlepoint suggests, "Anything worth doing is worth overdoing." I particularly like this one, because it gives me permission to overdo. And I do. I like movies, and if time permits, I might hit three in one day. I've been known to dance until my feet were almost falling off...sing until I have no voice left...laugh until I can't breathe... eat too much...sleep too much...whatever. I am not given to moderation. At the same time, I tend to apply that over-doing in all phases of my life. I want to do the best work, be the most thoughtful friend, etc. Sometimes, Larry has to remind me that moderation is a virtue, too.*

### LARRY ADDS:

*"I first learned this when my dad gave me some advice when I left the house on my way to my first job. He said when you have finished what you are supposed to do, "Pick up a broom." I realized as I*

*progressed in my career that what he was telling me was when I completed what I was expected to do, DO MORE.*

There is always something more to do. Write down **"Pick Up A Broom"** and you'll never forget this vital lesson in staying out of the way of your growth.

Staying out of your way can become a new habit, an exciting new paradigm, when we adopt the thinking that Wallace Wattles set forth in one of the chapters in <u>The Secret Science of Getting Rich</u>. Wattles talks about giving more in **Use Value** than **Cash Value**. Do more than what you're paid to do and offer more in Use Value for the Cash Value you receive.

Remember, living the life you want to have; growing from Survival to Success to Significance requires *effort* not *struggle*.

Step 5:

# Stay Out of Your Way

## A. Continuous Growth

Positive effort with total commitment is the formula for you to stay out of your way of success. Change the way you talk and eliminate what Marshall Sylver calls "wimp words" from your vocabulary. You may also find that when you change the way you speak it also affects how you *think.*

Let's look at a few basic wimp words:

**But**. No more "buts." Whenever you say BUT, it negates everything you said before. Substitute BUT with AND. Sure there are going to be challenges AND I will overcome them. The word AND allows you to focus on the solution; the word BUT causes stress, upset and sticks you where you are. Let's look at an example:

*"I would like to go shopping today, but I need to work on this manuscript."*

Wow. What a drag. I'd *much rather* go shopping. So now I'm resisting sitting here and working, when my mind is on shopping. In fact, the more I think about it, the more resentful I am. My head starts in with, *"You've been writing for several hours; you deserve a break."*

How about, instead, *"I would like to go shopping today, **and** I need to work on this manuscript."* Okay. That's the way it is. Now my mind can get busy on possibilities instead of being stuck in upset. *"Okay, I think I will work the rest of the day, then head over to the mall this evening and do some shopping - maybe even grab dinner."* Now I'm excited. And I haven't wasted any time or energy on upset or resentment. See the difference? Try it in your life and see if you can't eliminate some stress with this easy formula.

**HOPE** is not a strategy. How would you feel if you went to the doctor and he told you he *hoped* that the surgery you needed would be a success? I don't *think* so.

Substitute the word KNOW for HOPE. Be positive and confident and people will get it; perhaps one of those people might even be you. (Remember the old song from <u>The King and I</u>, *"Whistle a Happy Tune?"*)

**TRY** is one of our favorite examples of wimp words. We love it when people say they are going to try to do something. Try means they aren't going to do it. There is no state of trying; try is not an action verb.

Here's an exercise that might clarify this:

Ask someone to try to take from you a pen that you're holding. When they take it say, *"I didn't say take it, I said **try**."* They will return it to you and pretend that they're trying to take it. You admonish, *"No, you're not really trying. Really try to take it."* They will take it again. *"No, I didn't say take it; TRY to take it."* You'll see them hesitate and look very baffled. You've just demonstrated that there is no such *action* as "trying."

***Trying is not doing.***

When someone tells me they'll try, we say, *"I understand that you will try; however, will you or won't you do it?"*

## B. WIN WIN with GOOD Vibrations

We have heard about WIN-WIN strategies; it's nothing new. What is important is that it works. Win-Win is accomplished by sending out good vibrations, "good vibes" if you're from the '60s generation. When there are good vibrations, everyone feels that they have gained something and want to give even more.

### LARRY SHARES:

*Just before my mom passed away we talked to her regarding selling the family summer cottage that she'd owned since I was 8 years old. It was a traumatic decision, since my brother and I grew up there, as did our children. There were hard ties to surrender. We showed the cottage several times, and Mom would periodically change her mind as to whether she really wanted to sell.*

*Finally, one day, a young family came to look at*

*it. They were going to purchase it with a cousin and they all had young children. All of a sudden, Mom let us know that it would be okay to sell it to them if they wanted it. What changed for her? I am convinced that it was because family traditions and good feelings would be carried on even though she wouldn't own it anymore, and it wouldn't be our family. The new owners even gave Mom an open invitation to visit whenever she wanted. Good vibrations, a win-win? Absolutely.*

Have a WIN in your mind for whomever you deal with, and you'll get a WIN back. As Wallace Wattles says, *"It is all part of the Laws of Nature; the Laws of Cause and Effect."*

Some believe that negatives will come back to you faster than positives and that may be true. However, we'd like to give you a way to experience "The Law of Cause and Effect" in a positive way and have it come back to you immediately. The next time you go out to eat, just as the waitperson approaches your table, say, *"What is your name, and how can I help you?"* Remember, you have to say this before they say anything to you.

We assure you, you will experience some of the best service you have ever had. Do it today, and you'll see what we mean.

Saying positives will contribute greatly to your

staying out of your way; and it will contribute to others as well.

## C. NO Excuses Allowed

Eric Hofer once said, *"An excuse is better than achievement. That's because achievement, no matter how great, leaves you having to prove yourself again in the future. But an excuse can last for life."*

Don't make excuses. You are just getting in your way of achieving your dreams. Always aim for the greatest achievements you can imagine. You will find that those thoughts will flow into feelings and those feelings into actions and those actions into results and those results into reactions and those reactions into new thoughts. When all that starts out with **positive** thoughts, who knows how big our new dreams will be and what incredible realities we will experience?

George Bernard Shaw said, *"People are always blaming their circumstances for where they are. I don't believe in circumstances. The people who get on in this world are those who get up and look for the circumstances they want, and if they can't find then, make them."*

### Self Analysis

Use this as a self analysis. This is where you have to be totally honest with yourself in order to move on and get out of your own way. It's okay to acknowledge these negative aspects in your life. Acknowledging them and "owning" them is Step One in moving beyond them.

I talk to people about the things they put in their way; some of which, I also have put in my way. Are any of these in your way?

- Acne
- Alcohol abuse
- Apathy - futility syndrome
- Argumentativeness
- Arrogance
- Bad hair days
- Poorly or inappropriately dressed for success
- Not maximizing my physical attributes
- Not prioritizing activities
- Not taking responsibility for my own actions
- Not understanding my body and how it affects what I do
- Ineffective use of the 168 hours in the week
- Impoliteness
- Drug abuse
- Unreasonably high expectations for others
- "I'm always right" attitude
- "I'm better than that" attitude
- "I'm better than you" or "I'm not as good as you" attitude
- "I'm not good enough" attitude
- "It won't work for me" or "Nothing ever works for me" attitude

- Lack of education
- Laziness
- Low self esteem or self respect
- No plans or goals
- Body piercing in places that distract people
- Poor speech skills
- Pregnancy too young
- Relying on others to do things for me
- Relying on social programs
- Sarcasm
- Too much accent

Be responsive and not reactive. You now know what you have to work on, and now you have the tools to begin that journey.

Make of list of what would serve you to get where you want to be. What changes must you make?

**MARILYN SHARES:**
*I know two women, each facing an overweight issue. Each also wanted to have attractive acrylic fingernails. Woman #1 got her fake nails, which made her feel so much better about herself and so much more attractive, she then lost weight. She was experiencing herself as being attractive, so what happened was another action that increased how she already felt.*

*Woman #2 decided she would lose the weight and then reward herself with the nails. The second woman never lost the weight and still does not feel attractive. The first woman not only lost the weight, but also began to think of herself as attractive immediately. Remember BE-DO-HAVE?*

Final reminders:

1. Accept total responsibility for who, what and where you are.

2. Reevaluate your paradigms.

3. Identify your goals, values.

4. Prioritize your time.

5. Accept your fear…and rename it.

6. Visualize your success.

7. Commit to your goals.

8. Do tasks correctly and completely.

9. Act like a winner, talk like a winner.

10. Share your success and support others achieving success.

Remember, YOU are in charge. You are a powerful, successful person. Assuming we only go around once in this life, we invite you to "grab for all the gusto you can get." Now, NOW is the only time you can **act.** If you're afraid of looking silly or foolish, ask yourself this: How foolish will I look if I don't act? If you're afraid of failing, understand this: if you *don't* act, you've *already* failed.

There is plenty of money and plenty of happiness out there. We want you to share in it and enjoy it, too. We'd love to hear of your successes. Contact us through our website <u>www.getoutofyourwaynow.com</u>.

Now get out of your way and on your way!

Lots of love, happiness and success,

*Marilyn and Larry Singer*

# Acknowledgements

We are not PhD's or world scholars. We have read a lot about being motivated; taken numerous trainings offering enlightenment and rational living and spoken with many leaders in social sciences. We want to share and give credit to some of those whom we have studied and who have contributed to our realizations: thank you EST (Erhard Seminars Training); Tony Robbins; Zig Ziegler; Marshall Sylver; The Secret; Thomas Freese's <u>Secrets of Question Based Selling</u>; and Piet Hein's <u>Grooks</u> - for making it clear that we get in our own way, and that *each of us can do something about it.*

We would also like to thank our son, Harrison, for his continual, loving support and encouragement, and for his insightful and perceptive suggestions and painstaking edits for this book. He is an amazing young man.

Finally, we want to acknowledge the continual support of our colleague, KathySue Dorey Pohrte. She keeps us organized, sane, solvent and laughing. Her enthusiasm for - and help with - any and every new idea or new project we present is motivational…her sensible and creative input always right on target. Most of all, her friendship is invaluable. We are so fortunate to have her on our team.

P.S.

Just for fun, we have shared below some of our other favorite, sometimes provocative quotes that continually motivate us and get us back on track as needed.

*"Do not wish to be anything but what you are, and try to be that perfectly."*

- St. Francis De Sales

*"We are what we repeatedly do. Excellence, then, is not an act but a habit."*

- Aristotle

*"The ultimate victory in competition is derived from the inner satisfaction of knowing that you have done your best and that you have gotten the most out of what you had to give."*

- Howard Cosell, Sports Broadcaster

*"I am a big believer in the mirror test: all that matters is if you can look in the mirror and honestly tell the person you see there, that you've done your best."*

- John McKay, Football Coach

*"People forget how fast you did a job, but they remember how well you did it."*

- Anonymous

*"Small opportunities are often the beginning of great enterprises."*

- Demosthenes

*"The price of greatness is responsibility."*

- Winston Churchill

*"Man's mind, once stretched by a new idea, never regains its original dimensions."*

- Oliver Wendell Holmes

*"The future belongs to those who believe in the beauty of their dreams."*

- Eleanor Roosevelt

*"Don't wait for your ship to come in, swim out to it."*

- Anonymous

*"Unless you try to do something beyond what you have already mastered you will never grow."*

- Anonymous

*"I do the best I know how, the very best I can;*

*and I mean to keep on doing it to the end.*

*If the end brings me out all right,*

*What is said against me will not amount to anything.*

*If the end brings me out all wrong,*

*Ten angels swearing I was right would make no difference."*

- Abraham Lincoln

*"One ship drives east*

*And another west*

*With the self-same winds that blow:*

*'Tis the set of the sail and not the gale*

*Which determines the way they go.*

*As the winds of the sea are the ways of fate*

*As we voyage along through life,*

*'Tis the act of the soul that determines the goal,*

*And not the calm or the strife."*

- Ella Wheeler Wilcox

Now…Be on your way.

CPSIA information can be obtained at www.ICGtesting.com
Printed in the USA
LVOW100254190112

264565LV00006B/31/P

9 781432 723897